REACH GATHER GROW

IN COLOSSIANS

WRITTEN BY
PASTOR NOBLE BAIRD
& DR. RANDY T. JOHNSON

OUTLINED BY DR. RANDY T. JOHNSON
EDITED BY JEANNIE YATES
DESIGNED BY LORENA HABER
FORMATTED BY SHAWNA JOHNSON

Reach Gather Grow in Colossians

Copyright © 2023 by The River Church

Published by The River Church
          8393 E. Holly Rd.
          Holly, MI 48442

No part of this book may be reproduced or transmitted in any form or by any means, electronic or mechanical, including photocopying, recording or by any information storage and retrieval system, without the written permission of The River Church. Inquiries should be sent to the publisher. All rights reserved.

First Edition, August 2023

Printed in the United States of America

Unless otherwise marked, scripture quotations are taken from The Holy Bible, English Standard Version® (ESV®) Copyright © 2001 by Crossway, a publishing ministry of Good News Publishers. All rights reserved.

Scripture quotations marked (NKJV) are taken from The Holy Bible, New King James Version® Copyright © 1982 by Thomas Nelson.

Scripture quotations marked (NASB) are taken from The Holy Bible, New American Standard Bible® (NASB®) Copyright © 1960, 1971, 1977, 1995, 2020 by The Lockman Foundation. All rights reserved.

Scripture quotations marked (NLT) are taken from The Holy Bible, New Living Translation, Copyright © 1996, 2004, 2015 by Tyndale House Foundation. All rights reserved.

CONTENTS

9	**LESSON ONE · JOIN THE TEAM**
15	Devotion 1: Unshakable
17	Devotion 2: Laziness is Overrated
19	Devotion 3: Steadfast in Prayer
21	Devotion 4: Tychicus
23	Devotion 5: Mark
25	Devotion 6: Epaphras
29	**LESSON TWO · COLOSSIANS INTRODUCTION**
37	Devotion 1: Laugh!
39	Devotion 2: Mature in Christ
41	Devotion 3: Colossians 1
45	Devotion 4: Colossians 2
47	Devotion 5: Colossians 3
49	Devotion 6: Colossians 4
53	**LESSON THREE · REACH**
61	Devotion 1: Faith, Love, Hope
63	Devotion 2: Delivered
65	Devotion 3: Your Story
67	Devotion 4: We Were Dead
69	Devotion 5: Put Implies Action
71	Devotion 6: 525,960
75	**LESSON FOUR · GATHER**
83	Devotion 1: Phantom Pain
85	Devotion 2: When Life is Not Fair
87	Devotion 3: We Miss You
89	Devotion 4: Holding Fast to the Head
91	Devotion 5: Self-Made Religion
93	Devotion 6: And be Thankful
97	**LESSON FIVE · GROW**
105	Devotion 1: Pray for Knowledge
107	Devotion 2: Firm Foundation
109	Devotion 3: Captive
111	Devotion 4: Set Your Minds
113	Devotion 5: Proof is in the "Putting"
115	Devotion 6: Love

PREFACE

In Matthew 28:19-20, Jesus commands the mission for the church, ***"Go therefore and make disciples of all nations, baptizing them in the name of the Father and of the Son and of the Holy Spirit, teaching them to observe all that I have commanded you. And behold, I am with you always, to the end of the age."*** Some of Jesus' last words on Earth were for His followers to spread the Gospel, gather together for worship, and grow together in spiritual maturity.

In the book of Colossians, Paul follows these same guidelines as he directs the church in Colossae to Reach, Gather, and Grow. It is challenging and at the same time comforting to see the several examples in Colossians of how Paul strives to implement Jesus' mission for His church.

"Reach Gather Grow in Colossians" contains five study guides for personal or group discussion and thirty devotions for further insight. *"Reach Gather Grow in Colossians"* will remind you of the importance of your role as part of the church and will help you view the book of Colossians from a new and fresh perspective.

LESSON ONE

JOIN THE TEAM

DR. RANDY T. JOHNSON

Join The Team (JTT) is the opportunity of being part of something bigger than yourself. It is the calling of God to be involved with other believers in serving the Lord. Although it is a high calling, it is still a calling to all believers.

1. What teams were you on in school or other?

_____
_____
_____

2. What are some positive elements of being part of a team?

_____
_____
_____

We accept Jesus as Savior by faith. However, faith should be followed by actions. We do not serve in order to get to Heaven; we serve as a thank you to God because we are going to Heaven.

3. What does it mean to be "saved by faith"?

_____
_____
_____

4. What Bible verses support your answer?

_____
_____
_____

God not only calls us to serve, but He also equips us. God has given gifts, talents, skills, and interests to His children.

5. Apart from what God has given, what is one of the best gifts you remember receiving from someone?

_____
_____
_____

6. What is the greatest compliment you can give someone who gives you a gift?

_____

_____

_____

When we get someone a gift and see them value it, life is good. When children play with the toy instead of the box, the parents feel a sense of pride in a job well done. All too often people choose to store it away or regift it. I can only imagine our thoughts and feelings if we received a gift from someone that we had once given to another. I think it is fair to say that gifts are meant to be used.

One year when I was coaching boys high school varsity soccer, I had four freshmen make the starting line-up. That was very unique. I told them if I was going to coach them for four years that I wanted to show them how God could use what they loved to do for His glory. I took the soccer team to Mexico to frame a church building. The team was fabulous. Several times the missionary told us to take a break because he did not want to finish the project too soon (we could only be in the village as long as we were building). I asked about pulling out a soccer ball to kick around. He denied the request every time. Finally, he got frustrated with me and said, "I don't know what your view of ministry is, but mine is not to play. By the way, they don't even know what soccer is." I pointed out that the children were already playing soccer. He did not notice because they were using a two-liter bottle since they could not afford a real ball. He conceded to five minutes, but only five minutes.

As soon as we pulled out the soccer ball, everyone started yelling for the ball. Surprisingly, men showed up. The missionary had not met the men of the village. The men challenged my guys to a game and invited us to their "field" down by the water. The missionary gave his approval. The game went well. Friendships were created. We were able to share the Gospel with 128 men plus women and children. Many hands went up signifying that they had accepted Christ as their Savior. It was amazing. The boys played well and were invited to play neighboring teams. We even had to take boats to get to an island to play a select team.

We all learned God could use what we love to do for His glory. I ended up making fourteen more trips with students to Mexico. Every time the missionary requested that we play soccer.

7. What are some areas of service that are needed in or through the church? Please list at least 30.

_____
_____
_____

8. What are some of your interests and how can they be used for God's glory? (Ask the group for suggestions on how to use your skills and interests.)

_____
_____
_____

As a child, I feared if I gave my life to Jesus that He would send me to Africa to a place that did not even have baseball. Maybe you had similar thoughts. However, I realized that it would not make sense for God to place an interest, skill, talent, and even gift in me that He did not want to use for His glory.

Please grab the tools of your trade and Join the Team. We want you and need you.

"As each has received a gift, use it to serve one another, as good stewards of God's varied grace." 1 Peter 4:10

NOTES

UNSHAKABLE
DEVOTION #1 - PASTOR NOBLE BAIRD

"Therefore, as you received Christ Jesus the Lord, so walk in him, rooted and built up in him and established in the faith, just as you were taught, abounding in thanksgiving." Colossians 2:6-7

I am by no means a gardener. The closest I have ever come was an experiment in high school biology class - which I am pretty sure I failed! However, the concept of being rooted and growing roots is an essential part of growth and endurance. Paul writes in Colossians 2:6-7, *"Therefore, as you received Christ Jesus the Lord, so walk in him, rooted and built up in him and established in the faith, just as you were taught, abounding in thanksgiving."* Paul begins with the essential foundation of our faith, receiving Jesus Christ as Lord and Savior. It is acknowledging His sacrifice on the cross for our sins, burial, and glorious resurrection, through which we are saved and reconciled to the Lord! Yet it does not stop there. Once we receive Christ, we become His children as we are reminded in John 1:12. Not only His children, but we enter into an incredible family and team of believers, our brothers and sisters in Christ.

This is where the roots come in. We must grow. We must desire to walk in the words of Christ, not simply sit and receive knowledge - but to truly live it out. Then as we actively seek Him, grow in Him, encourage others, and challenge one another in Him, those roots deepen. Our foundation in Him becomes stronger, our roots are spread deeper, and when the difficulty of this world hits, we are unshaken because of the foundation and family around us.

So, as you continue in your day, ask yourself, "Am I rooted?" Are you truly growing, allowing the Word to penetrate your life so that you did not simply receive the Lord out of a case of fear or desire to be a part of a special team? Hopefully, you are truly allowing His word to grow in you, allowing it to take action in your life, and locking arms with your heavenly family to be rooted together and grow together in Him.

LAZINESS IS OVERRATED
DEVOTION #2 - PASTOR NOBLE BAIRD

"Whatever you do, work heartily, as for the Lord and not for men, knowing that from the Lord you will receive the inheritance as your reward. You are serving the Lord Christ." Colossians 3:23-24

Who are you working for? This may seem like a trivial and simple question. However, I want to take a look at Colossians 3:23-24, then as ourselves that question again. Paul writes in Colossians 3:23-24, *"Whatever you do, work heartily, as for the Lord and not for men, knowing that from the Lord you will receive the inheritance as your reward. You are serving the Lord Christ."* 2020 was a radical year for our world to say the least. I can remember clearly, the day Michigan was given the order to shut down schools and limit gatherings on March 13, 2020. It was a very confusing, scary, and concerning day. Yet, the Lord provided, and here we are in 2023 on the other side of that day.

I know that there are a lot of mixed feelings that can come up and be rushing around when we talk about that day and the days, weeks, and months that followed. However, one thing that was developed and produced out of that was laziness. It is laziness in our marriages, school, work, church, fitness, and relationships. Every company shifted to more readily available content at our leisure and fingertips. Whether it was working from home, having food delivered to your home, or watching church online, laziness began to creep in and it honestly even took place in my own life!

Sadly, this mentality and comfortability of laziness still have ramifications to this day. In churches all across the nation, we have seen a huge decline in not only physical attendance but also serving.

Serving and the urgency to serve together have gone to the wayside in our walks with the Lord. However, Paul challenges this notion of laziness here in Colossians 3:23-24. He reminds us that in all we do (in our marriages, work, school, relationships, life goals, and church) we are to serve no one except Him.

I want to ask you again, who are you working for? Are you working for yourself, a teacher, a boss, a paycheck, or a spouse? Ultimately, we are called to work heartily for no one and nothing else except the Lord. The goal is that in all we do we are glorifying Him and giving Him our absolute best. I truly believe with this mindset and reminder, today we can attack those moments and roots of laziness and turn back to serving, working, and glorifying an audience of One!

STEADFAST IN PRAYER
DEVOTION #3 - PASTOR NOBLE BAIRD

> *"Continue steadfastly in prayer, being watchful in it with thanksgiving. At the same time, pray also for us, that God may open to us a door for the word, to declare the mystery of Christ, on account of which I am in prison - that I may make it clear, which is how I ought to speak."* Colossians 4:2-4

At our Holly location, we began a time for "Prayer with Pastor" at 10:00 AM every Sunday since September of 2022. There are many things that I have had the privilege to see and be a part of during my time in ministry, but this one really took me by surprise. To see a group of 15-40 people come together every Sunday morning before the gathering for one thing – prayer is humbling. Prayer is not only foundational to our walk and relationship with Christ, it is essential! If you have not already prayed today, stop right now. Yes, literally stop reading this and pray.

Paul finishes up his letter to the church in Colossae, I believe intentionally, with a call to prayer. He writes in Colossians 4:2-4, **"Continue steadfastly in prayer, being watchful in it with thanksgiving. At the same time, pray also for us, that God may open to us a door for the word, to declare the mystery of Christ, on account of which I am in prison."** I love how Paul does not simply say pray, he calls us to be steadfast in our prayer with the Lord. We see this word used continually throughout the Word of God because it is truly a reminder that our walk with the Lord must be one of intentional endurance that does not cease or waiver. Not only are we called to be steadfast in our prayers, but we are called to be thankful. Oftentimes, we can find ourselves in a place of praying situationally. Prayer is used for times of need, distress, confusion, or hurt. Whereas Paul's closing remarks are to be watchful in our prayers to keep thanksgiving as a crucial part of our prayer lives.

After that, Paul takes the opportunity to ask for prayer for Timothy and him. I love this because this is what we as followers of Christ, brothers and sisters in the Lord, are called to do - pray for one another! This is why I love our prayer time before every gathering in Holly so much. It is family coming together in Christ, to thank Him for all He has done, to pray for our gathering that the Lord be glorified, and to pray for one another. It is my hope that we as a church, as His body, would be steadfast in our prayers, that we would continually thank Him in all circumstances, and that we would always be praying for and seeking opportunities to pray for one another!

TYCHICUS
DEVOTION #4 - DR. RANDY T. JOHNSON

"Tychicus will tell you all about my activities. He is a beloved brother and faithful minister and fellow servant in the Lord." Colossians 4:7

At the end of Paul's letters, he sends greetings from others who are serving with him. We often do the same thing when on the phone. If I am talking with one of our children, I might say, "Mom sends her love." I also send her greeting to friends, "By the way, Angela says, 'Hi!'"

A difference in Paul's greetings is that there are times when he describes the person who he is relaying the message from. In Colossians 4:7, he describes Tychicus, **"He is a beloved brother and faithful minister and fellow servant in the Lord."** The tendency can be to just pass over these phrases; however, it appears there is a message within them.

First, Paul calls Tychicus **"a beloved brother."** We would assume Tychicus was a believer, so Paul does not just call him a **"brother."** He is more than a Christian acquaintance. He is **"a beloved brother."** There is give and take in their relationship. When one is down, the other is there to pick him back up. We all have relationships that are one-sided. We feel we do all the giving. They only reach out when they need something. The conversation is always about them. That is not friendship; they are a project. Tychicus was different. He was **"a beloved brother."**

Second, Paul calls Tychicus **"a faithful minister."** In Ephesians 6:21, Paul also uses the same first two descriptions, **"Tychicus the beloved brother and faithful minister in the Lord will tell you**

everything.” Tychicus was a ***"faithful minister."*** He preached the Word. He knew, lived, and preached the Gospel. Paul could count on him. He was reliable, trustworthy, and dependable. He was a ***"faithful minister."***

Third, Paul calls Tychicus a ***"fellow servant in the Lord."*** This phrase caught my attention. I do not think Paul is being redundant. He is emphasizing that Tychicus is capable of being on stage sharing the Gospel. However, he does not strive to be the center of attention. Tychicus is also a ***"fellow servant."*** He is willing to do whatever it takes for others to hear the Good News.

Fellow servants are important. They do not get or need recognition. They just want to make a difference with their life. They want to serve the Lord. Their ministry is crucial! What they do helps set the tone or atmosphere for someone else to relax without distractions and hear the Gospel. These fellow servants work in the nursery, stand in corners making sure everyone is safe, pull weeds, run a camera, pick up garbage, straighten chairs, vacuum, change the oil in buses, clean windows, pray before gatherings and throughout the week, host Growth Communities, write to our missionaries, make hospital visits, and send notes of encouragement. Their ministry is crucial!

The mindset of a ***"fellow servant"*** says, "Just put me in the game, coach." It is the attitude of wanting to be involved in what God is doing. Please join the team. It is an honor and privilege to serve the Lord. The church needs faithful ministers and fellow servants. Together the message becomes all about Him. To God be the glory!

MARK
DEVOTION #5 - DR. RANDY T. JOHNSON

"Aristarchus my fellow prisoner greets you, and Mark the cousin of Barnabas (concerning whom you have received instructions - if he comes to you, welcome him)." Colossians 4:10

Paul references Mark and calls him *"the cousin of Barnabas."* Labels can make us feel of less importance. I remember interviewing for a job in front of a board of men when one of them said, "I am done." I did not know what I said. He then replied, "You are TJ's son?" I acknowledged the same. He then went on to make some compliments about my dad and therefore felt I would be a good addition to the team. Of course, I wanted to get the job on my own merits, but am thankful for my dad's reputation. I imagine you have been introduced as your child's parent or the sibling of a brother or sister. These labels often take the attention away from us.

Mark is more than just *"the cousin of Barnabas."* He served with Paul; however, there is more to the story. Acts 15:36-40 records, *"And after some days Paul said to Barnabas, 'Let us return and visit the brothers in every city where we proclaimed the word of the Lord, and see how they are.' Now Barnabas wanted to take with them John called Mark. But Paul thought best not to take with them one who had withdrawn from them in Pamphylia and had not gone with them to the work. And there arose a sharp disagreement, so that they separated from each other. Barnabas took Mark with him and sailed away to Cyprus, but Paul chose Silas and departed, having been commended by the brothers to the grace of the Lord."* Paul and Barnabas served together in many places. Others came with them. In this one instance, Barnabas wanted to bring Mark, but Paul refused.

Something happened on a previous missionary journey that made Paul feel he could not trust Mark anymore. Barnabas (which means **"son of encouragement"**) wanted to give Mark another chance. Paul and Barnabas parted ways. Paul decided to travel with Silas. Barnabas took Mark.

I do not know if you have had a bad experience in the past. I know that believers do not always live as they should. You might not have been given the position or opportunity that you know you deserved. If so, I am sorry to hear that. Please do not be mad at God because someone else ignored, snubbed, or walked all over you. Maybe the situation was not someone else's fault. It might be that you failed. Please do not let Satan use past hurts or failures to keep you from serving the Lord. Start again. Get involved.

Fortunately, Mark's story does not end there. He served again and was found faithful. We see him referenced in Colossians as being with Paul and called out in 2 Timothy 4:11, **"Luke alone is with me. Get Mark and bring him with you, for he is very useful to me for ministry."** Mark had a bad first quarter, few frames, or a couple of innings, but when the game was on the line, Paul said, **"Get Mark!"** Mark did not pout, quit, or take his ball and go home. He persevered. He pressed forward. The past was over. Now he was known as someone who **"is very useful to me for ministry."**

Own your past. Learn from it. Evaluate your gifts and skills. Join the team. You are needed. God's plan for you is not over. He is willing to do mighty things through you for His glory. God is good!

EPAPHRAS
DEVOTION #6 - DR. RANDY T. JOHNSON

"Epaphras, who is one of you, a servant of Christ Jesus, greets you, always struggling on your behalf in his prayers, that you may stand mature and fully assured in all the will of God."
Colossians 4:12

It was 1994. I had just finished teaching and was leaving for the day. I noticed one of my senior students sitting by himself. I checked in and found out he was feeling really down. He had recently dedicated his life to the Lord and wanted to be used by Him, but did not feel he had anything to offer. I asked what he loved to do. He replied with skateboarding. I suggested we try to find a way to use that. He did not think it was a good idea. I asked what would happen if I tried to reach that group with the Gospel. He replied, "They would not listen to you. You can't relate. You don't talk like them, dress like them. It wouldn't work." I smiled and asked who could reach them. A lightbulb went off.

In Colossians 4:12, Paul sends greetings from Epaphras to the Colossians, but he also makes an interesting observation about him. He says that Epaphras **"is one of you."** Epaphras was a Colossian. He could relate to them. He understood their culture.

Colossians 1:7 makes an interesting point, **"Just as you learned it from Epaphras our beloved fellow servant. He is a faithful minister of Christ on your behalf."** The Colossians heard the Gospel from Epaphras. It was not Paul who took the Good News to them. It was Epaphras. He reached his own neighborhood. He reached out to his people. Paul then came alongside him to minister further to them.

God can use anyone. It is often more about our availability than our ability. Each one of us has a group that we can better communicate with than others can. I am a city boy. It does not mean that I cannot talk to the rural community, but country people appreciate and understand country people. Hunters know hunting lingo. People who raise more than just a dog find common ground with others who also like to have horses, cows, pigs, ducks, chickens, and maybe even camels. Skateboarders get skateboarders.

You are needed. Please join the team. God's design is not to have the Pastor be the only one who talks to others. It is about a team. Each one is to reach one. I love having several locations because it allows people to reach their community for the Lord. Who has God placed in your little world that you can reach out to?

LESSON TWO
COLOSSIANS INTRODUCTION

PASTOR NOBLE BAIRD

"He has delivered us from the domain of darkness and transferred us to the kingdom of his beloved Son, in whom we have redemption, the forgiveness of sins." Colossians 1:13-14

All my life, I have been able to remember little random facts or moments in my life vividly; others are much more difficult. One of those moments was back in high school, sitting in Bible class and discussing the New Testament. We were going over the Epistle Letters written by Paul and my teacher told us, "Great Electric Power Company." For some, this is just a random phrase, but for me, it is a little phrase that has helped me to this day in remembering the order for four of Paul's letters: Galatians, Ephesians, Philippians, and Colossians.

1. Are there any phrases or acronyms you use to help remember things in God's Word?

_____
_____
_____

As we begin our journey through this letter that Paul wrote to the church in Colossae, I want to first encourage you to stop and pray. Pray that the Lord would not only prepare your heart but also that He would reveal something new or something that maybe has been avoided and now is the time to respond.

Colossians, we know from the opening verses, is a letter that was written by the Apostle Paul and Timothy, ***"Paul, an apostle of Christ Jesus by the will of God, and Timothy our brother, to the saints and faithful brothers in Christ at Colossae: Grace to you and peace from God our Father"*** (Colossians 1:1-2). Timothy is often referred to as Paul's son, brother, and co-author for much of Paul's ministry. I have always loved and admired Paul and Timothy's relationship. Their desire to share the Gospel is what brought them together and through the highs and lows of life and ministry, they sharpened one another and continued to do life and ministry together to the end! It is believed that Paul wrote this letter while under house arrest in Rome which places this letter being penned around 60-62 AD.

2. Do you have a "Timothy" or are you a "Timothy" to a "Paul" in your life?

_____
_____
_____

As the letter continues in this first chapter, we learn some important facts about the church. First, we learn of their love and faith in the Gospel, **"We always thank God, the Father of our Lord Jesus Christ, when we pray for you, since we heard of your faith in Christ Jesus and of the love that you have for all the saints, because of the hope laid up for you in heaven. Of this you have heard before in the word of the truth, the gospel, which has come to you, as indeed in the whole world it is bearing fruit and increasing - as it also does among you, since the day you heard it and understood the grace of God in truth"** (Colossians 1:3-6). Second, we learn that their pastor, and the one who shared the message of the Gospel to those in Colossae, was Epaphras, **"Just as you learned it from Epaphras our beloved fellow servant. He is a faithful minister of Christ on your behalf and has made known to us your love in the Spirit"** (Colossians 1:7-8). Third, we learn that the church is actively sharing the Good News of Christ and they are being sanctified by the Spirit, **"Because of the hope laid up for you in heaven. Of this you have heard before in the word of the truth, the gospel, which has come to you, as indeed in the whole world it is bearing fruit and increasing - as it also does among you, since the day you heard it and understood the grace of God in truth"** (Colossians 1:5-6).

3. In Colossians 1:3-6, Paul and Timothy write about the Gospel that the Colossians had received and believed. Take some time to share what the Gospel is and share passages of Scripture to walk through it.

_____

_____

_____

Paul then takes an important step in this introduction by encouraging them, but he also challenges the church. Beginning in verse 9 we read, *"And so, from the day we heard, we have not ceased to pray for you, asking that you may be filled with the knowledge of his will in all spiritual wisdom and understanding, so as to walk in a manner worthy of the Lord, fully pleasing to him: bearing fruit in every good work and increasing in the knowledge of God; being strengthened with all power, according to his glorious might, for all endurance and patience with joy; giving thanks to the Father, who has qualified you to share in the inheritance of the saints in light. He has delivered us from the domain of darkness and transferred us to the kingdom of his beloved Son, in whom we have redemption, the forgiveness of sins."* It is so encouraging to see Paul and Timothy's devotion to not only prayer, but praying for their brothers and sisters in Christ. Can you imagine how our daily lives would change and how the life of the church would change, if we too did not cease praying for one another? The first encouragement and challenge we have from Paul and Timothy is prayer. They are encouraging the church by letting them know that since they received word from Epaphras of the church's faith, they have not ceased to pray for them. Then, we have a list of four specific areas which are being prayed for and the church is challenged to grow and emulate in their walk with Christ: bear fruit, gain knowledge of the Lord, be steadfast, and be patient. They are to endure and give thanks for the gift of eternity through Christ.

4. It seems as if Epaphras reached into the lives of those in Colossae and shared the Gospel of Christ with them. Who is the Epaphras in your life who shared the Gospel with you?

_____
_____
_____

5. What does the word sanctification mean? What has that looked like in your life?

_____
_____
_____

Finally, Paul takes the opportunity in the final verses of chapter 1 to address a growing issue of deception with the doctrinal truth of Christ. Gnosticism was a growing heretical belief during this time. It was one that Paul had heard, and I am sure seen, during his travels, as a growing issue. At the core, and still to this day, this belief system believes that there is a kind of a god; however, one can access and become more spiritual and somehow attain a higher level closer to God by their own doing and acts. There is no faith in Jesus is as God, nor that He is the Messiah. Jesus is not viewed as the one true way to our Heavenly Father. Therefore, Paul writes a truly beautiful and glorifying passage about Christ's supremacy and deity. Beginning in verse 15 he writes, ***"He is the image of the invisible God, the firstborn of all creation. For by him all things were created, in heaven and on earth, visible and invisible, whether thrones or dominions or rulers or authorities - all things were created through him and for him. And he is before all things, and in him all things hold together. And he is the head of the body, the church. He is the beginning, the firstborn from the dead, that in everything he might be preeminent. For in him all the fullness of God was pleased to dwell, and through him to reconcile to himself all things, whether on earth or in heaven, making peace by the blood of his cross. And you, who once were alienated and hostile in mind, doing evil deeds, he has now reconciled in his body of flesh by his death, in order***

to present you holy and blameless and above reproach before him, if indeed you continue in the faith, stable and steadfast, not shifting from the hope of the gospel that you heard, which has been proclaimed in all creation under heaven, and of which I, Paul, became a minister" (Colossians 1:15-23). I hope you took the time to truly read Paul's words about Jesus. Honestly, I would encourage you to read it again. There is so much doctrinal and biblical truth packed into these verses that I do not want you to miss! Jesus is the beginning and the end. He is the Alpha and the Omega. He has always been there from the very beginning and He forever will be. He is alive and active this very second in His glorious resurrected body! He is the truth, and the Gospel on which we stand is through Him alone. He is how we have life and gain access to our Heavenly Father.

6. What part of Colossians 1:15-23 sticks out to you?
_____
_____
_____

As we begin this journey over the next couple weeks into the book of Colossians, I pray that we do so with the mindset of Colossians 1:15-23 as the foundation for this entire study. No matter what we go through, the highs, lows, valleys, storms, and times of peace and rejoicing, may we never forget the amazing Savior we serve and His love and desire for us.

Knowing that Colossians is a letter written to the church, have you read it as a letter? Most letters we read in one sitting. There would be no chapter or verse breaks. Simply read Colossians like a letter as it was written.

NOTES

LAUGH!
DEVOTION #1 - DR. RANDY T. JOHNSON

> *"And so, from the day we heard, we have not ceased to pray for you, asking that you may be filled with the knowledge of his will in all spiritual wisdom and understanding, so as to walk in a manner worthy of the Lord, fully pleasing to him: bearing fruit in every good work and increasing in the knowledge of God."*
> Colossians 1:9-10

I have heard of and was raised with a number of rules in church. There can be certain dress codes (which include no hats for the guys). Hair had to be a certain way. Tattoos were a no-no. Music (especially drums) had made its way into some church doctrinal statements. However, I recently read an article that had possibly the worst one yet – no laughing in church. It appears to some, laughing shows disrespect to God. Is anyone with me wondering about the joy of the Lord?

As we start our study on the book of Colossians, I wanted to point out one of the purposes of the letter. Paul wanted to show the superiority of Christ over all human philosophies and traditions.

Norman Geisler wrote that Paul "sought to show the deity and supremacy of Christ in the face of the Colossian heresy (1:18; 2:9)." It is believed that heresy includes legalism. In his commentary writing, Peter O'Brien observed the same thing, "The young converts were under external pressure to conform to the beliefs and practices of their Jewish and pagan neighbors." Warren Wiersbe agrees saying, "What was the heresy that threatened the peace and purity of the Colossian church? It was a combination of Eastern philosophy and Jewish legalism, with elements of what Bible scholars call Gnosticism."

Legalism is dangerous. It makes man the judge. Pause and think about that. It adds to Scripture, which is very scary. It focuses on man instead of Christ and works instead of the grace of God. Commentator Thomas Schreiner wrote, "Legalism exists when people attempt to secure righteousness in God's sight by good works. Legalists believe that they can earn or merit God's approval by performing the requirements of the law."

I started with Colossians 1:9-10 because of the phrase **"walk in a manner worthy of the Lord, fully pleasing to him."** Our actions should not distract others from coming to the Lord, but at the same time, others should not judge based on outward appearance. This coming Sunday (and every day), focus on pleasing the Lord, and feel free to laugh.

MATURE IN CHRIST
DEVOTION #2 - DR. RANDY T. JOHNSON

"Him we proclaim, warning everyone and teaching everyone with all wisdom, that we may present everyone mature in Christ." Colossians 1:28

Maturity is an interesting topic. The passing of years makes one older but not necessarily more mature. Maturity takes intentional growth. Oswald Chambers states it this way, "Spiritual maturity is not reached by the passing of the years, but by obedience to the will of God."

Paul wrote to combat legalism (yesterday's topic), but another topic was to **"present everyone mature in Christ."** Paul focused on **"warning everyone and teaching everyone."** He proclaimed Christ and they needed to be humble, teachable, and willing to change. I like how Billy Graham described it, "The goal of a child's life is maturity - and the goal of a Christian's life is spiritual maturity."

It is a lengthy quote, but I like how preacher and theologian Charles Spurgeon (1834-1892) describes maturity, "We shall, as we ripen in grace, have greater sweetness towards our fellow Christians. Bitter-spirited Christians may know a great deal, but they are immature. Those who are quick to censure may be very acute in judgment, but they are as yet very immature in heart. He who grows in grace remembers that he is but dust, and he therefore does not expect his fellow Christians to be anything more; he overlooks ten thousand of their faults, because he knows his God overlooks twenty thousand in his own case. He does not expect perfection in the creature, and, therefore, he is not disappointed when he does not find it... I know we who are young beginners in grace think ourselves qualified to reform the whole Christian church. We drag her before us, and condemn her straightway; but when our virtues become more mature, I trust we shall not be more tolerant of evil, but we shall be more tolerant of infirmity, more hopeful for the people of God, and certainly less arrogant in our criticisms."

Paul also addresses maturity in Colossians 2:6-7, **"Therefore, as you received Christ Jesus the Lord, so walk in him, rooted and built up in him and established in the faith, just as you were taught, abounding in thanksgiving."** These words describe the effort by the teacher and student. I like how Paul adds thanksgiving to the list of walking, rooted, built up, and established. It is the proper response. Again, maturity and growth must be intentional.

Max Lucado closes this section well, "God never said that the journey would be easy, but He did say that the arrival would be worthwhile."

COLOSSIANS 1
DEVOTION #3 - ESV

<u>Greeting</u>

Paul, an apostle of Christ Jesus by the will of God, and Timothy our brother,

To the saints and faithful brothers in Christ at Colossae:

Grace to you and peace from God our Father.

<u>Thanksgiving and Prayer</u>

We always thank God, the Father of our Lord Jesus Christ, when we pray for you, since we heard of your faith in Christ Jesus and of the love that you have for all the saints, because of the hope laid up for you in heaven. Of this you have heard before in the word of the truth, the gospel, which has come to you, as indeed in the whole world it is bearing fruit and increasing—as it also does among you, since the day you heard it and understood the grace of God in truth, just as you learned it from Epaphras our beloved fellow servant. He is a faithful minister of Christ on your behalf and has made known to us your love in the Spirit.

And so, from the day we heard, we have not ceased to pray for you, asking that you may be filled with the knowledge of his will in all spiritual wisdom and understanding, so as to walk in a manner worthy of the Lord, fully pleasing to him: bearing fruit in every good work and increasing in the knowledge of God; being strengthened with all power, according to his glorious might, for all endurance and patience with joy; giving thanks to the Father, who has qualified you to share in the inheritance of the saints in light. He has delivered us from the domain of darkness and transferred us to the kingdom of his beloved Son, in whom we have redemption, the forgiveness of sins.

The Preeminence of Christ

He is the image of the invisible God, the firstborn of all creation. For by him all things were created, in heaven and on earth, visible and invisible, whether thrones or dominions or rulers or authorities—all things were created through him and for him. And he is before all things, and in him all things hold together. And he is the head of the body, the church. He is the beginning, the firstborn from the dead, that in everything he might be preeminent. For in him all the fullness of God was pleased to dwell, and through him to reconcile to himself all things, whether on earth or in heaven, making peace by the blood of his cross.

And you, who once were alienated and hostile in mind, doing evil deeds, he has now reconciled in his body of flesh by his death, in order to present you holy and blameless and above reproach before him, if indeed you continue in the faith, stable and steadfast, not shifting from the hope of the gospel that you heard, which has been proclaimed in all creation under heaven, and of which I, Paul, became a minister.

Paul's Ministry to the Church

Now I rejoice in my sufferings for your sake, and in my flesh I am filling up what is lacking in Christ's afflictions for the sake of his body, that is, the church, of which I became a minister according to the stewardship from God that was given to me for you, to make the word of God fully known, the mystery hidden for ages and generations but now revealed to his saints. To them God chose to make known how great among the Gentiles are the riches of the glory of this mystery, which is Christ in you, the hope of glory. Him we proclaim, warning everyone and teaching everyone with all wisdom, that we may present everyone mature in Christ. For this I toil, struggling with all his energy that he powerfully works within me.

COLOSSIANS 2
DEVOTION #4 - NKJV

Not Philosophy but Christ

For I want you to know what a great conflict I have for you and those in Laodicea, and for as many as have not seen my face in the flesh, that their hearts may be encouraged, being knit together in love, and attaining to all riches of the full assurance of understanding, to the knowledge of the mystery of God, both of the Father and of Christ, in whom are hidden all the treasures of wisdom and knowledge.

Now this I say lest anyone should deceive you with persuasive words. For though I am absent in the flesh, yet I am with you in spirit, rejoicing to see your good order and the steadfastness of your faith in Christ.

As you therefore have received Christ Jesus the Lord, so walk in Him, rooted and built up in Him and established in the faith, as you have been taught, abounding in it with thanksgiving.

Beware lest anyone cheat you through philosophy and empty deceit, according to the tradition of men, according to the basic principles of the world, and not according to Christ. For in Him dwells all the fullness of the Godhead bodily; and you are complete in Him, who is the head of all principality and power.

Not Legalism but Christ

In Him you were also circumcised with the circumcision made without hands, by putting off the body of the sins of the flesh, by the circumcision of Christ, buried with Him in baptism, in which you also were raised with Him through faith in the working of God, who raised Him from the dead. And you, being dead in your trespasses and the uncircumcision of your flesh, He has made alive together with Him, having forgiven you all trespasses, having wiped out the handwriting of requirements that was against us, which was contrary to us. And He has taken it out of the way, having nailed it to the cross. Having disarmed principalities and powers, He made a public spectacle of them, triumphing over them in it.

So let no one judge you in food or in drink, or regarding a festival or a new moon or sabbaths, which are a shadow of things to come, but the substance is of Christ. Let no one cheat you of your reward, taking delight in false humility and worship of angels, intruding into those things which he has not seen, vainly puffed up by his fleshly mind, and not holding fast to the Head, from whom all the body, nourished and knit together by joints and ligaments, grows with the increase that is from God.

Therefore, if you died with Christ from the basic principles of the world, why, as though living in the world, do you subject yourselves to regulations— "Do not touch, do not taste, do not handle," which all concern things which perish with the using— according to the commandments and doctrines of men? These things indeed have an appearance of wisdom in self-imposed religion, false humility, and neglect of the body, but are of no value against the indulgence of the flesh.

COLOSSIANS 3
DEVOTION #5 - NASB

<u>Put On the New Self</u>

Therefore, if you have been raised with Christ, keep seeking the things that are above, where Christ is, seated at the right hand of God. Set your minds on the things that are above, not on the things that are on earth. For you have died, and your life is hidden with Christ in God. When Christ, who is our life, is revealed, then you also will be revealed with Him in glory.

Therefore, treat the parts of your earthly body as dead to sexual immorality, impurity, passion, evil desire, and greed, which amounts to idolatry. For it is because of these things that the wrath of God is coming upon the sons of disobedience, and in them you also once walked, when you were living in them. But now you also, rid yourselves of all of them: anger, wrath, malice, slander, and obscene speech from your mouth. Do not lie to one another, since you stripped off the old self with its evil practices, and have put on the new self, which is being renewed to a true knowledge according to the image of the One who created it— a renewal in which there is no distinction between Greek and Jew, circumcised and uncircumcised, barbarian, Scythian, slave, and free, but Christ is all, and in all.

So, as those who have been chosen of God, holy and beloved, put on a heart of compassion, kindness, humility, gentleness, and patience; bearing with one another, and forgiving each other, whoever has a complaint against anyone; just as the Lord forgave you, so must you do also. In addition to all these things put on love, which is the perfect bond of unity. Let the peace of Christ, to which you were indeed called in one body, rule in your hearts; and be thankful. Let the word of Christ richly dwell within you, with all wisdom teaching and admonishing one another with psalms, hymns, and spiritual songs, singing with thankfulness in your hearts to God. Whatever you do in word or deed, do everything in the name of the Lord Jesus, giving thanks through Him to God the Father.

Family Relations

Wives, be subject to your husbands, as is fitting in the Lord. Husbands, love your wives and do not become bitter against them. Children, obey your parents in everything, for this is pleasing to the Lord. Fathers, do not antagonize your children, so that they will not become discouraged.

Slaves, obey those who are your human masters in everything, not with eye-service, as people-pleasers, but with sincerity of heart, fearing the Lord. Whatever you do, do your work heartily, as for the Lord and not for people, knowing that it is from the Lord that you will receive the reward of the inheritance. It is the Lord Christ whom you serve. For the one who does wrong will receive the consequences of the wrong which he has done, and that without partiality.

COLOSSIANS 4
DEVOTION #6 - NLT

Masters, be just and fair to your slaves. Remember that you also have a Master—in heaven.

An Encouragement for Prayer

Devote yourselves to prayer with an alert mind and a thankful heart. Pray for us, too, that God will give us many opportunities to speak about his mysterious plan concerning Christ. That is why I am here in chains. Pray that I will proclaim this message as clearly as I should.

Live wisely among those who are not believers, and make the most of every opportunity. Let your conversation be gracious and attractive so that you will have the right response for everyone.

Paul's Final Instructions and Greetings

Tychicus will give you a full report about how I am getting along. He is a beloved brother and faithful helper who serves with me in the Lord's work. I have sent him to you for this very purpose—to let you know how we are doing and to encourage you. I am also sending Onesimus, a faithful and beloved brother, one of your own people. He and Tychicus will tell you everything that's happening here.

Aristarchus, who is in prison with me, sends you his greetings, and so does Mark, Barnabas's cousin. As you were instructed before, make Mark welcome if he comes your way. Jesus (the one we call Justus) also sends his greetings. These are the *only Jewish believers among my co-workers; they are working with me here for the Kingdom of God. And what a comfort they have been!*

Epaphras, a member of your own fellowship and a servant of Christ Jesus, sends you his greetings. He always prays earnestly for you, asking God to make you strong and perfect, fully confident that you are following the whole will of God. I can assure you that he prays hard for you and also for the believers in Laodicea and Hierapolis.

Luke, the beloved doctor, sends his greetings, and so does Demas. Please give my greetings to our brothers and sisters at Laodicea, and to Nympha and the church that meets in her house.

After you have read this letter, pass it on to the church at Laodicea so they can read it, too. And you should read the letter I wrote to them.

And say to Archippus, "Be sure to carry out the ministry the Lord gave you."

HERE IS MY GREETING IN MY OWN HANDWRITING—PAUL.

Remember my chains.

May God's grace be with you.

LESSON THREE
REACH

PASTOR NOBLE BAIRD

"By canceling the record of debt that stood against us with its legal demands. This he set aside, nailing it to the cross."
Colossians 2:14

Years ago, I was given the opportunity to go down to the streets of Atlanta, Georgia for a mission trip. Our goal was twofold. First, was to meet the physical needs of the homeless on the streets and in shelters. Second, was to share the Gospel as opportunities arose. While the trip itself was life-changing for me on so many levels, one lesson that has impressed my life ever since was when the director of the organization we partnered with told us not to return. Our first reaction was utter confusion. Had we done something wrong? Did we mess up our presentation of the Gospel? Had we offended someone on the streets? The director went on to share with us a passage from Acts 1:8. Jesus says, **"But you will receive power when the Holy Spirit has come upon you, and you will be my witnesses in Jerusalem and in all Judea and Samaria, and to the end of the earth."** The director then told us, this is not your **"Jerusalem."** He was right. We were a small youth group from Michigan just above Detroit. He challenged us to go back home and reach out to those in the communities the Lord had placed us in, to truly be a witness of the Gospel there.

1. Have you ever had the chance to go on a mission trip before? What was that experience like?
___
___
___

2. Where is your Jerusalem?
___
___
___

3. What does it mean to be a witness and could you say that you are truly being the witness that we all have been called to, by Christ, in Acts 1:8?

_____

_____

_____

In Colossians chapter 2, Paul continues his letter by encouraging the church to four specific areas of growth, but also foundational practices which they must daily take on. Paul writes in Colossians 2:6-7, **"Therefore, as you received Christ Jesus the Lord, so walk in him, rooted and built up in him and established in the faith, just as you were taught, abounding in thanksgiving."** Paul's heart and desire for not only the church, but for those of us who are followers of Christ, is continually his concern for their spiritual well-being. That is why so often, he will challenge and encourage at the same time a call to action after one has accepted Jesus as Lord and Savior. Paul lays out these four action steps that must be carried out in order that **"no one may delude you with plausible arguments"** (Colossians 2:4). The first three actions Paul calls us to are a call to remember the Gospel message which has saved us, a call to continually live in light of the Gospel and to grow in our knowledge and understanding of Him. Paul writes, **"rooted and built up in him and established in the faith."** Jesus gives the parable in Matthew chapter 13 about the seed falling into four different types of soil. The first, fell on the ground and was taken away by the birds. The second, fell by a rock bed; therefore, it did not have any depth or true root system to take ground. The third, had its roots choked out by the thorns and things of the world. Therefore, those roots also never took real depth and growth. It is only the fourth seed that took root and grew.

4. When you read the parable of the four soils, are there things in your life that may be choking the roots of the Lord from growing and producing fruit?

_____
_____
_____

Paul is calling us to truly be rooted in Christ. If we have truly accepted that free gift of the Gospel, we must allow His Word and His will to take root in our lives daily. Therefore, being built up and established in Christ is the natural progression as we deepen our relationship with Him. Finally, Paul gives a call to thanksgiving. Again, we see this reminder in many of Paul's letters to the churches. Honestly, for a man who went through so much hardship and suffering in his life and ministry, I cannot help but believe that he wrote this not only as a reminder to us but to himself as well! Paul uses the word **"abounding"** here, talking about an overflow that outweighs the circumstances of this world, and focuses back on that foundational truth of the goodness of the Gospel. In 1 Thessalonians 5:18, Paul takes this a step further saying, **"Give thanks in all circumstances; for this is the will of God in Christ Jesus for you."** Again, this daily reminder that Paul undoubtedly needed, and so do we, is to abound in our thanksgiving of the Gospel. It is then to trust and remain faithful in all circumstances of this world!

5. When was the last time you stopped and truly thanked the Lord for all He has done?

_____
_____
_____

Paul continues his letter, encouraging the church of their faith, but to also be on guard. In Colossians 2:8-15, he writes, **"See to it that no one takes you captive by philosophy and empty deceit, according to human tradition, according to the elemental spirits of the world, and not according to Christ. For in him the whole fullness of deity dwells bodily, and you have been filled** *in him, who is the head of all rule and authority. In him also you were circumcised with a circumcision made without hands, by putting off the body of the flesh, by the circumcision of Christ, having been buried with him in baptism, in which you were also raised with him through faith in the powerful working of God, who raised him from the dead. And you, who were dead in your trespasses and the uncircumcision of your flesh, God made alive together with him, having forgiven us all our trespasses, by canceling the record of debt that stood against us with its legal demands. This he set aside, nailing it to the cross. He disarmed the rulers and authorities and put them to open shame, by triumphing over them in him."* Along with his continual reminder of thankfulness to the Lord, Paul was continually concerned for the spiritual safeguards of the believer. The way in which he does this is by first dispelling the lies of philosophical rhetoric, lofty speech, and gnostic spiritualism. He continues on in Colossians 2:16-22, warning of submitting to and being held captive by the lies of the world and human teaching and precepts, as Paul refers to them. Instead, He reminds them of the Gospel. It is the simple and profound truth of Christ and what He did. That truth of the cross and resurrection culminates beautifully in verses 13-14, *"And you, who were dead in your trespasses and the uncircumcision of your flesh, God made alive together with him, having forgiven us all our trespasses, by canceling the record of debt that stood against us with its legal demands. This he set aside, nailing it to the cross."* That is what the Gospel is all about and ultimately what this thing called "Reach" is about. Jesus took on our record of debt, our sin, and our penalty upon Himself. He was crucified on our behalf, carrying the sin of the world on His shoulders, so that we could live.

6. Who is one person that you can be praying for that the Spirit would move in their heart to soften them to the message of the Gospel?

_____
_____
_____

7. What are some passages of Scripture that can be used to walk through and explain what the Gospel truly is?

_____
_____
_____

Our debt has been paid. The cross was and is enough. God so loved us that He sent His Son Jesus to pay the penalty for our sins. However, He did not stop there because He arose victoriously conquering death, Hell, and the grave! That is what "Reach" is all about, the true Gospel of Christ.

NOTES

FAITH, LOVE, HOPE
DEVOTION #1 - DR. RANDY T. JOHNSON

"We always thank God, the Father of our Lord Jesus Christ, when we pray for you, since we heard of your faith in Christ Jesus and of the love that you have for all the saints, because of the hope laid up for you in heaven. Of this you have heard before in the word of the truth, the gospel." Colossians 1:3-5

Three words jump out in this passage – faith, love, and hope. In 1 Corinthians 13:13, Paul writes, **"So now faith, hope, and love abide, these three; but the greatest of these is love."** Norman Geisler ties these three words together well, "Faith is the soul looking upward to God; love looks outward to others; hope looks forward to the future. Faith rests on the past work of Christ; love works in the present; and hope anticipates the future." These words (faith, love, hope) are central to reaching others for Christ.

I think it is good to pause and ponder after reading about the **"hope laid up for you in heaven."** Slow down. You probably have several things you are waiting to do and another dozen that will pop up as the day goes along. Some of the items are good but a number of them could bring some stress. Some of the items you might even dread. However, no matter how tough things seem right now, there is still hope. It is such an important topic that we find the word "hope" 76 times in the New Testament. Romans 8:18 captures this sentiment, **"For I consider that the sufferings of this present time are not worth comparing with the glory that is to be revealed to us."** That **"glory"** is the **"hope laid up for you in heaven."** You might be asking, "How should I do this?" Romans 12:12 gives a practical answer, **"Rejoice in hope, be patient in tribulation, be constant in prayer."**

Finally, Paul reminds us of the foundation being ***"the word of the truth, the gospel."*** Faith, love, hope, and glory are all possible because of the Gospel. That truly is Good News!

DELIVERED
DEVOTION #2 - DR. RANDY T. JOHNSON

"He has delivered us from the domain of darkness and transferred us to the kingdom of his beloved Son, in whom we have redemption, the forgiveness of sins." Colossians 1:13-14

Is it more important to realize what you are saved from or what you are saved to? If one is drowning, they just want to get out of the water. They do not care if it is a boat, raft, driftwood, or an inflated pink flamingo pool float. The focus is on what they are saved from. I understand the awe-inspiring thoughts of Heaven, but we need to remember what we are saved from. We are saved from Hell, the Lake of Fire, **"the wrath of God"** (Romans 5:9), and as it is described here, **"the domain of darkness."**

The concept is so strong that Paul says Christ has **"delivered us."** As believers in Christ, we are freed, liberated, released, and rescued from Satan's grip. We have been delivered. We now need to help deliver others. Our goal is stated in 2 Corinthians 2:11, **"So that we would not be outwitted by Satan; for we are not ignorant of his designs."** We must help others escape Satan's **"designs"** (ESV), **"schemes"** (NIV, NLT), or **"devices"** (KJV, NKJV). Satan lays a trap, and we need to help family and friends avoid it or be delivered.

After using the word **"delivered,"** Paul speaks about **"redemption."** The two words are similar. Today, we understand what it means for someone to be delivered. In the first century, they would have understood the word redemption. It meant to be bought with a price. It was more than just delivering someone, it included paying a price. They were rescued from slavery because someone paid a price – they were redeemed. Jesus Christ paid the price for us!

This passage in Colossians then ends with **"the forgiveness of sins."** The fact that we need to be delivered is our own fault. We have sinned. We sold our souls to Satan, but Jesus bought us back with His death on the cross. We are redeemed. Not only are we free, but we are forgiven. When we give our lives to the Lord, we are delivered, redeemed, and forgiven. This last part means He will not use it against us. All too often couples bring up past flaws in the heat of a fight. They know what buttons to press. God does not do that. He says, "You are forgiven." Accept the forgiveness from the Heavenly Father and walk confidently in and toward Him.

YOUR STORY
DEVOTION #3 - DR. RANDY T. JOHNSON

"And you, who once were alienated and hostile in mind, doing evil deeds, he has now reconciled in his body of flesh by his death, in order to present you holy and blameless and above reproach before him, if indeed you continue in the faith, stable and steadfast, not shifting from the hope of the gospel that you heard, which has been proclaimed in all creation under heaven, and of which I, Paul, became a minister." Colossians 1:21-23

I am blessed. I was raised in a Christian home. My mom was a "bus kid." She and her older sister went out by the street when they were just out of kindergarten. My grandparents did not go, but they let the girls hop on a bus to church and eventually hear and heed the Gospel. My dad accepted Christ in his late teens at a Billy Graham crusade. Therefore, I was raised in a Christian home, going to church, having morning devotions, and praying together. The concept of a "Loving Father" made sense to me and I accepted Christ as Savior at age seven. I was baptized at age twelve, rededicated my life to Christ in 10th grade, and felt the call to ministry while still in high school.

Although I accepted Christ early, I was a sinner in need of as much salvation as any murderer. I am thankful God saved me early in life and protected me from many scars.

This Colossians passage gives every believer's story. We *"were alienated and hostile in mind"* which Jesus saved *"by his death"* and made us *"holy and blameless."* It is by *"faith"* and is *"the hope of the gospel."* A testimony consists of what we were, what He did, and who we are now.

The readers knew Paul's story. He killed Christians, met Jesus, repented, obeyed Jesus, and **"became a minister."** He went from Saul to Paul.

What is your story? Think through the details. Who did God use to point you to Jesus? Did God use an event in your life that seemed horrible but He turned it into something beautiful?

Ephesians 2:13 says, **"But now in Christ Jesus you who once were far off have been brought near by the blood of Christ."**

WE WERE DEAD
DEVOTION #4 - DR. RANDY T. JOHNSON

"And you, who were dead in your trespasses and the uncircumcision of your flesh, God made alive together with him, having forgiven us all our trespasses, by canceling the record of debt that stood against us with its legal demands. This he set aside, nailing it to the cross. He disarmed the rulers and authorities and put them to open shame, by triumphing over them in him." Colossians 2:13-15

Prison ministry can be very rewarding. When talking about the Gospel, you do not normally have to spend much time on Romans 3:23, **"For all have sinned and fall short of the glory of God."** They understand sin. They have experienced it and live with it every day. That is sort of refreshing as opposed to someone at work or school who feels they are good enough or not as bad as a drug dealer or murderer. I wonder why they never compare themselves to Billy Graham or Mother Theresa.

In Colossians chapter 2, Paul points out that you (and me) **"were dead in your trespasses."** I am not sure we realize how bad this is. Death is used as an analogy for something bad. We could not do anything about it. We had a price we could not pay. We were hopeless and lost.

However, check all the phrases Paul uses about what God has done for us:

- *"God made alive"*
- *"Forgiven us all our trespasses"*
- *"Canceling the record of debt"*
- *"He set aside"*

- *"Nailing it to the cross"*
- *"He disarmed"*

God is alive and active in our lives. He has, is, and will do so much for us. We need to pause and thank Him. We then need to thank Him again, and again.

This passage reminds me of the Prodigal Son as recorded in Luke chapter 15. The son wants to live for himself. He rejects a relationship with his father and lives for himself. Eventually, he realizes he is doomed and does not have a chance of survival. In despair, he humbly comes back to his father. The father celebrates his son's choosing to have a relationship with him.

This is true with the Heavenly Father. We are self-serving and until we realize our hopeless situation, there is no hope. However, when we humbly come before Him, the Father rescues us. Luke 15:32 summarizes our situation, **"It was fitting to celebrate and be glad, for this your brother was dead, and is alive; he was lost, and is found."**

PUT IMPLIES ACTION
DEVOTION #5 - DR. RANDY T. JOHNSON

"Put to death therefore what is earthly in you: sexual immorality, impurity, passion, evil desire, and covetousness, which is idolatry. On account of these the wrath of God is coming. In these you too once walked, when you were living in them. But now you must put them all away: anger, wrath, malice, slander, and obscene talk from your mouth. Do not lie to one another, seeing that you have put off the old self with its practices and have put on the new self, which is being renewed in knowledge after the image of its creator." Colossians 3:5-10

Some words in Scripture can seem to be overlooked. The word *"put"* is used four times in this passage. Put implies action. As we are saved, we need to be active in our walk. Philippians 2:12 says, *"Therefore, my beloved, as you have always obeyed, so now, not only as in my presence but much more in my absence, work out your own salvation with fear and trembling."* We need to *"work out"* our salvation. This is for our growth but also as a testimony to others. Reaching others with the Gospel involves our talk and our walk. This is "Reach" through our walk.

- **Put to death** - We are to put to death *"sexual immorality, impurity, passion, evil desire, and covetousness."* These items can consume someone. Paul even references idolatry. They can cause someone or something other than God to rule our hearts and minds. Do not feed this animal.
- **Put away** - We are to put away *"anger, wrath, malice, slander, and obscene talk."* A lot of these deal with emotions that get out of control. Self-control is a sign of maturity. It is even listed as a Fruit of the Spirit.

- **Put off** - We are to put off *"the old self."* Paul isolates one sin of the old self – lying. That makes sense since God is the truth. His Word is truth. The other side is ruled by the Father of Lies. I have heard a lot of parents say to their children, "Just tell me what happened and we will deal with it. Just do not lie." The punishment was worse due to a lie.
- **Put on** - We are to put on *"the new self."* Paul said it another way in 2 Corinthians 5:17, *"Therefore, if anyone is in Christ, he is a new creation. The old has passed away; behold, the new has come."*

525,960
DEVOTION #6 - DR. RANDY T. JOHNSON

"Walk in wisdom toward outsiders, making the best use of the time. Let your speech always be gracious, seasoned with salt, so that you may know how you ought to answer each person."
Colossians 4:5-6

"Indeed" posted an interesting article, *"100 High-Paying Careers To Consider (With Average Salaries)."* I found the list interesting. The top 13 were all in the medical field headed by cardiologists making an average of $351,827 per year. Vice presidents are at $151,358 per year. Software architects average $139,127 per year. Pharmacy managers average $112,546. Midwives make $103,311. Attorneys average $89,487, while judges average $83,715 (that seemed a little backward). Salaries can be all over the spectrum and I did not even touch professional athletes or entertainers.

Although salaries vary, we all receive the same number of minutes each year – 525,960. No one can buy any more. The key is how we spend them. Colossians 4:5 puts out a strong challenge, **"Walk in wisdom toward outsiders, making the best use of the time."** It is important to God how we use our money, but it is equally important to how we spend our time. It is limited and you cannot bank it away for the future. Paul is very straightforward that how we spend our time is important as a witness **"toward outsiders."** Jesus could come at any time, they may not have long to live, and our days are numbered so we need to make the most of the time.

David Jeremiah says it well, "You may not be able to predict the time of a tornado, earthquake, or the Lord's return. But you can know for a fact that He is coming back. Work today to share the escape route of God's grace with others, before the night cometh." I love the imagery of an "escape route." We need to constantly remember the destiny of lost family, friends, neighbors, and co-workers. They need to be rescued by Christ and we can be part of the rescue team.

The mission of the church (Matthew 28:19-20) includes Reach, Gather, and Grow. Our growth is an integral part of reaching others with the Gospel. We need to study the Word so we are prepared to speak with an unbeliever. In Colossians 5:6, Paul says studying the Word is important **"so that you may know how you ought to answer each person."**

LESSON FOUR
GATHER

PASTOR NOBLE BAIRD

"And let the peace of Christ rule in your hearts, to which indeed you were called in one body. And be thankful." Colossians 3:15

Gathering by definition (according to Google) is "an assembly or meeting, especially a social or festive one or one held for a specific purpose." Gatherings have taken many different forms and agendas for many different people. For some, there are family gatherings that happen yearly or on holidays. For others, these gatherings can be with school friends or coworkers. Yet, one of the most important gatherings that we can prioritize in our lives is that of gathering together with our brothers and sisters in Christ. As we continue in this letter, Paul writes about the radical life change of the Gospel. Specifically, he shares how we have a holistic lifestyle and mindset change because of Christ's finishing work on the cross and His resurrection for our sins.

1. What are some gatherings that are a tradition for you or your family to attend?

_____
_____
_____

2. What does the phrase "gather with the saints" mean to you?

_____
_____
_____

In Colossians 3:1-3, we read, ***"If then you have been raised with Christ, seek the things that are above, where Christ is, seated at the right hand of God. Set your minds on things that are above, not on things that are on earth. For you have died, and your life is hidden with Christ in God."*** Paul begins with an ***"if then"*** statement that helps to set apart to whom these gathering of the saints pertains. Simply, it is those who have accepted Jesus Christ as their Lord and Savior. Yet, it does not end there. While it is truly confessing with our mouths and believing in our hearts that Jesus is Lord (Romans 10:9), there must be a radical holistic change that permeates every part of us. So, Paul says, **"Set your minds on things that are above, not on things that are on earth."** This is such an important mindset for us to desire and strive for as followers of Christ. However, what does that mean and then practically look like? First, Paul lays out the things that are on earth that we must not only walk away from but put to death. He continues in Colossians 3:5-11, *"Put to death therefore what is earthly in you: sexual immorality, impurity, passion, evil desire, and covetousness, which is idolatry. On account of these the wrath of God is coming. In these you too once walked, when you were living in them. But now you must put them all away: anger, wrath, malice, slander, and obscene talk from your mouth. Do not lie to one another, seeing that you have put off the old self with its practices and have put on the new self, which is being renewed in knowledge after the image of its creator. Here there is not Greek and Jew, circumcised and uncircumcised, barbarian, Scythian, slave, free; but Christ is all, and in all."*

3. What have you found in Christ that you were never able to find in the things of this world?

_____
_____
_____

4. Is there anything in Paul's list in Colossians 3:5-11 that you need to work on in your life?

_____
_____
_____

I believe that Paul purposely says to put these to **"death"** for a reason. Death is a very heavy word with much finality behind it. As followers of Christ, while we know death is real (Romans 6:23), death is only the beginning of life eternal with Christ our Savior! In this context, Paul uses death in regard to our sinful, worldly nature and our life before Christ. It is important to understand that if we truly accept Christ as our Lord and Savior, there must and will be a true change in our life. Since Paul put everyone in a great mood with our list of shortcomings and failures, he quickly follows us with this passage of encouragement of what the heavenly things above truly are. Colossians 3:12-17 says, **"Put on then, as God's chosen ones, holy and beloved, compassionate hearts, kindness, humility, meekness, and patience, bearing with one another and, if one has a complaint against another, forgiving each other; as the Lord has forgiven you, so you also must forgive. And above all these put on love, which binds everything together in perfect harmony. And let the peace of Christ rule in your hearts, to which indeed you were called in one body. And be thankful. Let the word of Christ dwell in you richly, teaching and admonishing one another in all wisdom, singing psalms and hymns and spiritual songs, with thankfulness in your hearts to God. And whatever you do, in word or deed, do everything in the name of the Lord Jesus, giving thanks to God the Father through him."**

5. Note the words **"thankful"** and **"thankfulness"** in this passage. When was the last time you thanked the Lord?

_____
_____
_____

One thing I admire about Paul is his desire and direction for action. He began in verse 5 saying, **"Put to death,"** and then he begins verse 12 with, **"Put on then."** The things above that Paul referenced earlier in this passage, he now gives a practical list for us to desire and strive for: holiness, compassion, kindness, humility, meekness, patience, love, and forgiveness. The list could continue on and on. At the end of the day, it is a list of everything that not only Christ taught, but that He lived out. As followers of Christ, we have been called to live it out, to focus on the things above, and to allow the Spirit of God to penetrate who we are so that we become more like Him. That is what the sanctification process is all about. It is becoming more and more like Christ daily.

6. Are you a team player or do you like to do things solo?

_____
_____
_____

However, there is the second half of this passage that is so essential to our lives as believers. Beginning in verse 15, **"And let the peace of Christ rule in your hearts, to which indeed you were called in one body. And be thankful. Let the word of Christ dwell in you richly, teaching and admonishing one another in all wisdom, singing psalms and hymns and spiritual songs, with thankfulness in your hearts to God."** We have been called to gather together as one body. When we accept Christ and enter into this new life, we are quite literally joining His team as we are a part of His family forever. Therefore, Paul lists the practices that we as a team are called to so that we can focus on the things above and not be distracted or overcome by the things of this world. So, what are these practices that we as the body have been called to? We have been called to gather together to read and hear from God's Word, to encourage and advise one another, to worship the Lord in congregational singing and praise, and to remind each other of thankfulness for the Lord's goodness in all things.

7. Why do you go to church?

_____
_____
_____

8. Is gathering a priority for you and your family or an inconvenience?

_____
_____
_____

I cannot tell you the number of times I have sat down with friends and people at church who have come to me saying that they are struggling with being at church. Every time I ask them why. I genuinely want to know their point of concern that is so great that it has brought them to the place of desiring to leave and go somewhere else. In the majority of cases, I hear the answer that either the messages that are being preached are not directed toward them, the music is not their "style," or the environment is not to their liking. Now, I will say there are times and situations of true concern and those people have left on good terms or we were able to discuss and understand the issue at hand. However, to those who felt like the church was not supplementing their spiritual, emotional, or theological needs; I always pose the question, "Are you at church to serve or be served?"

9. Do you go to church to serve or be served?

_____
_____
_____

The reality is that every message, every song, and every change will never be to our desires and growth one hundred percent of the time. Yet, if we heed the words of Paul and understand the design Christ set forth for gathering as the body, we will find peace, joy, growth, and excitement. Gathering is essential. The writer of Hebrews calls believers to gather together and not neglect this important time. So, as you continue this week, whatever day it may be or wherever you may attend church, I hope that you make it a priority to gather. I hope it is a weekly priority for you to be physically present with the body of Christ, worshiping, sharing in His Word, encouraging one another, and giving thanks for all He has done and continues to do for us!

10. What can you do this week to serve together as the body of Christ?

_____
_____
_____

NOTES

PHANTOM PAIN
DEVOTION #1 - DR. RANDY T. JOHNSON

"He is the image of the invisible God, the firstborn of all creation. For by him all things were created, in heaven and on earth, visible and invisible, whether thrones or dominions or rulers or authorities - all things were created through him and for him. And he is before all things, and in him all things hold together. And he is the head of the body, the church. He is the beginning, the firstborn from the dead, that in everything he might be preeminent." Colossians 1:15-18

This passage describes Jesus so well. He is God. He existed before all of creation. Actually, He created everything. It is all about Him. He is the boss. He even rose from the dead so others can. This is such a beautiful picture.

In describing so many details about Jesus, Paul points out that **"he is the head of the body, the church."** The concept of Jesus being the head of the body (the church) is not a new concept in Scripture (1 Corinthians 11:3; 12:12, 27; Romans 12:5; Colossians 1:24; 2:19; Ephesians 1:22; 4:15; 5:30). He is the source, chief, and leader. He is to be in charge.

These passages also mention His body, which is the church (all believers). As I was thinking through this passage, the concept of phantom pain came to mind. Phantom pain is when someone has a sense of pain even though the limb is missing. A friend of mine lost his left leg below the knee when he was in a car accident as a teenager. Even though it has been over 40 years, his left "foot" hurts or even itches from time to time.

In discussing church gatherings, I wonder how those who are "missing" send pain to the Head. Obviously, the loss of a limb affects the whole body, but the effect on the Head is most significant. Fortunately, those "missing" parts of the church can be reconnected and very useful.

Evaluate for yourself, "Are you connected to the body of Christ?" As you take your next step forward, remember how important each part of the body is.

WHEN LIFE IS NOT FAIR
DEVOTION #2 - DR. RANDY T. JOHNSON

"Now I rejoice in my sufferings for your sake, and in my flesh I am filling up what is lacking in Christ's afflictions for the sake of his body, that is, the church, of which I became a minister according to the stewardship from God that was given to me for you, to make the word of God fully known." Colossians 1:24-25

One of the most common questions among believers and those contemplating whether Christianity is true is, "Why do bad things happen to good people?" I think the opposite can be difficult too, "Why do good things happen to bad people?" Since none of us are actually good (Romans 3:23), we should count our blessings.

There are at least three reasons why struggles come into our life. First, choices have consequences. When we sin, we should expect to be disciplined. Deuteronomy 8:5 says, *"Know then in your heart that, as a man disciplines his son, the Lord your God disciplines you."* Hebrews 12:6 adds, *"For the Lord disciplines the one he loves, and chastises every son whom he receives."* Discipline is the natural outcome of a poor choice.

Second, difficulties may be allowed to come into our lives to strengthen us or to help us grow in our faith. Hebrews 12:10 says, *"For they disciplined us for a short time as it seemed best to them, but he disciplines us for our good, that we may share his holiness."* God disciplines us *"for our good."* It is to help us grow in holiness. James 1:2-4 says, *"Count it all joy, my brothers, when you meet trials of various kinds, for you know that the testing of your faith produces steadfastness. And let steadfastness have its full effect, that you may be perfect and complete, lacking in*

nothing." I must confess that ***"joy"*** is not always my first response. However, God gives us tests so we are more prepared for future exams. Breaking down a muscle can make it stronger.

Third, sometimes it is not about us. We might be allowed to suffer for the sake of others. In Acts chapter 16, Paul and Silas are beaten and thrown in prison for preaching the Gospel. They did not do anything wrong. However, because of their response in praising the Lord, others came to a saving knowledge. God allowed them to suffer knowing He could count on them to reach others with the Gospel. In 2 Corinthians 1:3-4, we read another aspect of how our suffering can help others, **"Blessed be the God and Father of our Lord Jesus Christ, the Father of mercies and God of all comfort, who comforts us in all our affliction, so that we may be able to comfort those who are in any affliction, with the comfort with which we ourselves are comforted by God."** God may allow us to go through something so that in the future we can empathize with someone else while pointing them to the Lord. Coming together for Gatherings allows us an opportunity to build each other up. Love is powerful when shared.

If you are presently struggling, do not immediately beat yourself up. Ask God how He can turn your mess into a message, your test into a testimony. Remember Paul's statement in the opening passage, ***"Now I rejoice in my sufferings for your sake."***

WE MISS YOU
DEVOTION #3 - DR. RANDY T. JOHNSON

"For though I am absent in body, yet I am with you in spirit, rejoicing to see your good order and the firmness of your faith in Christ." Colossians 2:5

I know there are people reading this devotion who due to health or their work schedule cannot attend church gatherings. They understand this verse and want to tell fellow believers, **"For though I am absent in body, yet I am with you in spirit."** Some of you now have more time to pray for others and send notes of encouragement. Please know, we miss you.

Some others have a different story. They got used to not attending church gatherings and liked the convenience of watching online whenever they desire. Hebrews 10:24-25 says, **"And let us consider how to stir up one another to love and good works, not neglecting to meet together, as is the habit of some, but encouraging one another, and all the more as you see the Day drawing near."** It is easy and dangerous to get into the habit of not attending church gatherings. Please break the habit. We want to encourage you and need your encouragement.

Paul missed attending church gatherings with friends in several places. He not only missed those in Colossae, but in Romans 1:8-12, he references wanting to see the believers in Rome, **"First, I thank my God through Jesus Christ for all of you, because your faith is proclaimed in all the world. For God is my witness, whom I serve with my spirit in the gospel of his Son, that without ceasing I mention you always in my prayers, asking that somehow by God's will I may now at last succeed in coming to you. For I long to see you, that I may impart to you some**

spiritual gift to strengthen you - that is, that we may be mutually encouraged by each other's faith, both yours and mine." While Paul is away, he is praying for them. However, he wants to get back to them to give and get. He wants ***"to strengthen"*** them, but also looks forward to being ***"mutually encouraged."***

The River Church is one church with multiple locations. It is a blessing that we can go to our website and find several sermons on the same topic in each series. However, this does not replace the interactive worship that takes place in person with one another.

If you cannot make it to a gathering, please keep in touch through the online presence. However, if you are able to attend, we welcome you back. We need you and you need us. We miss you.

HOLDING FAST TO THE HEAD
DEVOTION #4 - DR. RANDY T. JOHNSON

"Therefore let no one pass judgment on you in questions of food and drink, or with regard to a festival or a new moon or a Sabbath. These are a shadow of the things to come, but the substance belongs to Christ. Let no one disqualify you, insisting on asceticism and worship of angels, going on in detail about visions, puffed up without reason by his sensuous mind, and not holding fast to the Head, from whom the whole body, nourished and knit together through its joints and ligaments, grows with a growth that is from God." Colossians 2:16-19

In Colossians, Paul was challenging the believers about feeling defeated or distracted by man-made rituals. People were keeping score of how good or at least how much better they were than others (in their own minds). In the midst of this discussion, Paul points out that they are **"puffed up without reason."** Ephesians 2:8-9 discusses this dangerous mindset, **"For by grace you have been saved through faith. And this is not your own doing; it is the gift of God, not a result of works, so that no one may boast."** This is serious because when we focus on ourselves, we are not **"looking to Jesus, the founder and perfecter of our faith"** (Hebrews 12:2). It should always be all about Jesus. The second problem arises out of the first.

Some of the people were so focused on themselves that they were **"not holding fast to the Head."** In John 15:5, Jesus says it this way, **"I am the vine; you are the branches. Whoever abides in me and I in him, he it is that bears much fruit, for apart from me you can do nothing."** If we are not "plugged in" to the energy source, we are fruitless. Without fruit, we have lost our purpose.

My older sister passed away eight years ago. When she was fifteen months old she contracted Encephalitis. She medically died, but my father revived her. Although she physically grew, she never had the mind of one over ten months old. Encephalitis is inflammation of the brain; therefore, oxygen cannot get to the brain. My younger sister and I gained a special appreciation for those who are challenged in various ways. Medically, we learned that being separated from the head is deadly.

Spiritually, this is true. All too often believers think they can walk and even worship on their own. They feel they do not need the church or other believers. In essence, they become separated from the Head. The church is the body of Christ, but they dislocate themselves and can become **"puffed up without reason."**

Believers need the church and the church needs all believers. We all have gifts and talents that are needed by others. Every part of the body is important and needs to stay connected. As we gather together as the body of Christ, we grow **"with a growth that is from God"** (Colossians 2:19).

SELF-MADE RELIGION
DEVOTION #5 - DR. RANDY T. JOHNSON

"If with Christ you died to the elemental spirits of the world, why, as if you were still alive in the world, do you submit to regulations – 'Do not handle, Do not taste, Do not touch' (referring to things that all perish as they are used) - according to human precepts and teachings? These have indeed an appearance of wisdom in promoting self-made religion and asceticism and severity to the body, but they are of no value in stopping the indulgence of the flesh." Colossians 2:20-23

In Colossians, Paul was challenging the believers about feeling defeated or distracted by man-made rituals. In the Old Testament, God gave the Ten Commandments, but the Jewish rulers came up with 613 laws. I am sure the readers understood and had heard all too often the statement, **"Do not handle, Do not taste, Do not touch."** It must have felt like young parents with a toddler walking through the crystal section of a store.

Paul is blunt in his appraisal of the culture affecting these believers. He says they have the **"appearance of wisdom."** That may sound like a compliment, but it is not. It reminds me of the statement, "Better to remain silent and be thought a fool than to speak and to remove all doubt." In this case, the legalists had an **"appearance of wisdom,"** but their restrictive form of "worship" was foolish. It was not about Christ as it was a **"self-made religion."** That is the culture of today, too. People want to determine for themselves what is truth. They have no standard. They live by their emotions. They, in essence, have created their own church or religion. It is very similar to the book of Judges, **"Everyone did what was right in his own eyes"** (Judges 17:6; 21:25).

People have taken spiritual liberty to the point of selfishness. They avoid gatherings or only attend when it is convenient. They have become lazy and do not want to commit to serving in any way as something better may come along. Paul references this in Galatians 5:13, *"For you were called to freedom, brothers. Only do not use your freedom as an opportunity for the flesh, but through love serve one another."* Our liberty should not pull us away from believers.

God's design for worship does include the daily times when we are reminded to *"be still, and know that I am God"* (Psalm 46:10). However, there is great emphasis on corporate worship. They gathered together to worship. There is something about gathering with others as Matthew 18:20 says, *"For where two or three are gathered in my name, there am I among them."* Since He is with us always, He must be emphasizing the importance of gathering with others. He might be cheesy, but it is impossible to spell church without "u" (You!).

AND BE THANKFUL
DEVOTION #6 - DR. RANDY T. JOHNSON

"And let the peace of Christ rule in your hearts, to which indeed you were called in one body. And be thankful. Let the word of Christ dwell in you richly, teaching and admonishing one another in all wisdom, singing psalms and hymns and spiritual songs, with thankfulness in your hearts to God. And whatever you do, in word or deed, do everything in the name of the Lord Jesus, giving thanks to God the Father through him."
Colossians 3:15-17

This passage is filled with concepts associated with gatherings:

- One body
- Teaching
- Admonishing
- Sings psalms and hymns

However, one theme is repeated three times:

- *"And be thankful."*
- *"With thankfulness in your hearts"*
- *"And whatever you do, in word or deed, do everything in the name of the Lord Jesus, giving thanks to God the Father through him."*

The concept of a church gathering and being thankful should naturally go together. Going and being involved in a gathering is a way of saying thank you to God. This is a repeated theme. Psalm 100:4 says, **"Enter his gates with thanksgiving, and his courts with praise! Give thanks to him; bless his name!"** Please come to the gatherings excited to express thanks to God. Let others know how good He is. Psalm 111:1 adds, **"Praise the Lord! I will give thanks to the Lord with my whole heart, in the company of the upright, in the congregation."** He mentions that we should **"give thanks"** to the Lord while with other believers.

People ask, "What is God's will for my life?" In 1 Thessalonians 5:16-18, Paul gives an answer, **"Rejoice always, pray without ceasing, give thanks in all circumstances; for this is the will of God in Christ Jesus for you."** We are to be thankful.

Psalm 92:1 adds, **"It is good to give thanks to the Lord, to sing praises to your name, O Most High."** It is a little humorous how basic this statement is. He basically says, "In case you are wondering, it is a good thing to thank God." Sometimes powerful advice can be simple logic.

Going back to our original passage, I love the second sentence – **"And be thankful."** I am not sure English teachers would allow it structurally, but it sure says it all. We need to take time to intentionally and publicly thank God.

LESSON FIVE
GROW

PASTOR NOBLE BAIRD

By the time this book is printed, my son Archer will be almost two years old. Even writing that seems so crazy! The blessing it has been to simply watch him from birth to now leaves me amazed. He has gone from a little eight-pound three-ounce nugget, to well over twenty-four pounds at fifteen months alone. Seeing his growth has been amazing. He has gone from formula to pulling a plate with a slice of pizza onto the floor so that he can eat that piece of pizza faster! While I could literally go on and on with how blessed my wife and I are to raise our son, I cannot help but imagine the pride Paul felt as he wrote to many of these churches, especially the church in Colossae.

1. Can you share a special memory or story of growth for yourself or a loved one?

_____
_____
_____

As Paul wraps up his letter to the church, he desires continued growth in their maturity and walk with the Lord. Starting in Colossians 4:2, he writes, **"Continue steadfastly in prayer, being watchful in it with thanksgiving."** Without a doubt, one of the absolute essentials for growth and simply our walk with Christ is prayer. Prayer was an essential part of Christ's ministry and Paul urges the churches to prioritize and continue this practice. He echoes these words in 1 Thessalonians 5:17, **"Pray without ceasing."** While this is not a literal command to physically be in prayer 24 hours a day, this is a mindset and holistic communion with the Lord at the forefront of all we do in our lives.

2. When was the last time you prayed?

_____
_____
_____

3. Is prayer an essential part of your walk or just used in times of crisis or need?

_____

_____

_____

Again, Paul brings up the importance of thanksgiving. In Colossians 3:15 we were challenged to be thankful and again here in Colossians 4:2, he says it. If something is instructed once, we ought to learn and put it into practice; however, if something is instructed twice, it may be because that instruction is often overlooked and neglected. Thankfulness is a part of our walk and growth in the Lord that can take a back seat. We can get too busy with our supplications and requests to the Lord because of the immediacy at hand, that we completely forget to just say thank you for the work and blessings He has already done. Thankfulness must go hand in hand with our prayer life. I want to encourage you right now, to stop. Stop reading, stop discussing, and truly take a few minutes to pray and specifically thank God for what He has done for you and how He has blessed you.

Growth takes time. I am not sure about you, but this is a truth that I have had to learn over many years and am still learning. One of the most important practices in understanding this truth is patience. Paul continues this passage in Colossians 4:3-6, *"At the same time, pray also for us, that God may open to us a door for the word, to declare the mystery of Christ, on account of which I am in prison - that I may make it clear, which is how I ought to speak. Walk in wisdom toward outsiders, making the best use of the time. Let your speech always be gracious, seasoned with salt, so that you may know how you ought to answer each person."*
I love how while Paul is instructing, encouraging, and teaching the church, he gives them a practical task to begin right away. He asks the church that while they pray steadfastly, to be praying for him and the Gospel message which we all share and are called to proclaim.

4. When was the last time you truly set aside the time to earnestly thank the Lord for all He has given and done for you?

_____
_____
_____

5. What does spiritual growth look like?

_____
_____
_____

Paul wrote, **"Walk in wisdom toward outsiders."** This phrase is so essential for us as followers of Christ as we continue to grow in Him. The book of Proverbs is truly saturated in wisdom, as Solomon was led by the Spirit of God. We all know that being human, Solomon messed up! However, that is a part of growth. We will mess up. We will overlook opportunities, we will forget at times situations that have occurred or we have experienced, and yes, sin will creep in. Yet, by the grace of God and through Christ's finishing work on the cross and His glorious resurrection, we are forgiven! So, through those times when we mess up, we must acknowledge, seek forgiveness when needed, and grow from that situation. Then, looking back to the example of Solomon and the same calling that Paul is giving us here in Colossians chapter 4, seek wisdom from the Lord. Solomon writes in Proverbs 2:6, **"For the LORD gives wisdom; from his mouth come knowledge and understanding."** Also, in Proverbs 9:10 he writes, **"The fear of the LORD is the beginning of wisdom, and the knowledge of the Holy One is insight."**

6. What are some other passages of Scripture that speak of wisdom?

_____
_____
_____

7. When was the last time you asked and leaned on the wisdom of the Lord, instead of yourself?

_____

_____

_____

What does this talk about prayer, thanksgiving, and wisdom mean in relation to growth? First, the only way to truly grow in our relationship with Christ is by being in communion with Him. If I decide to go weeks on end without saying a word to my son, how will I build a relationship with him? I cannot! Yet, as followers of Christ, we expect our walk to grow and we expect Him to hear us when we go weeks and even months without talking to Him at all. So, in order to grow, we must first prioritize our prayer life. Second, we must be thankful - always. We live in a fast-food society as I call it. We want everything now, we just want, want, want, and expect it instantly or next-day delivery; however, we forget our manners. We forget to thank the Lord for all He has done, for His continued provision, especially in those situations when we do not understand. Paul reminds us of this truth of thanksgiving again in 1 Thessalonians 5:18, **"Give thanks in all circumstances; for this is the will of God in Christ Jesus for you."** As part of our spiritual growth and maturity, we must have a heart of thanksgiving in all circumstances to the Lord. Finally, we must seek the wisdom of the Lord. As followers of Christ, we have been tasked with reaching the world with the Gospel. Yet, in order to do this, we must wholistically be wise in all that we do, so that we can reflect that Gospel which has so radically changed each of us. Paul says in Colossians 4:5-6, to seek this wisdom so that we can be gracious and effective as we carry out this mission. Again, remember that wisdom does not come from the mouth of man, but from our Heavenly Father!

8. In what practical ways will you seek out spiritual growth this week, this month, or this year? (If you are struggling, please reach out to your Location Pastor or your Growth Community leader. We are in this together!)

_____
_____
_____

Remember, our growth and walk with the Lord are just that, a walk and not a race. I simply want to encourage you to continue to seek the Lord personally, but also together as a group and family because we should not try to do this life alone. Paul ends his letter by listing off several brothers and sisters in the Lord, who he has done life and ministry with, that are taking the Gospel to the world. He does this to encourage the church that they are not alone. We are all in this together. Rejoice in the work that is being done! Celebration is a huge part of growth. It is not only celebration but sharing in one another's struggles and hurts as well. No matter where you might be on your walk with the Lord, I hope that each day we are striving to grow closer to the Lord and simply reflect His Gospel to the world!

NOTES

PRAY FOR KNOWLEDGE
DEVOTION #1 - DR. RANDY T. JOHNSON

> *"And so, from the day we heard, we have not ceased to pray for you, asking that you may be filled with the knowledge of his will in all spiritual wisdom and understanding, so as to walk in a manner worthy of the Lord, fully pleasing to him: bearing fruit in every good work and increasing in the knowledge of God."*
> Colossians 1:9-10

When I wake up at night and cannot sleep, I pray. I first listen to see if God has placed someone on my heart. Often, I know some things I can pray for them, but not always. I might not sure what they are going through, but I can pray.

We tend to pray for health, finances, and relationships. This is good, but Paul prays for two other things in Colossians 1:9-10.

Pray *"that you may be filled with the knowledge of his will."*

Pray that they would know what God's plan for them is and that they would follow it. Philippians 1:9-10 says, *"And it is my prayer that your love may abound more and more, with knowledge and all discernment, so that you may approve what is excellent, and so be pure and blameless for the day of Christ."* People should seek the *"knowledge"* of God's *"excellent"* plan. Good is not good enough. In Romans 12:2, Paul again tells us to seek discernment in finding God's plan, *"Do not be conformed to this world, but be transformed by the renewal of your mind, that by testing you may discern what is the will of God, what is good and acceptable and perfect."* Good is not good enough when *"perfect"* is offered and expected.

Pray that you are *"increasing in the knowledge of God."*

We have the privilege to know God personally. Christianity is more than a religion; it is a relationship with God. A healthy relationship involves getting to know each other better. God knows everything about you and still loves you. Do you know Him? Peter, like Paul, emphasizes knowing God in 2 Peter 1:2, **"May grace and peace be multiplied to you in the knowledge of God and of Jesus our Lord."** Later, in 2 Peter 3:18, he adds, **"But grow in the grace and knowledge of our Lord and Savior Jesus Christ. To him be the glory both now and to the day of eternity. Amen."** A very important aspect of growing in our faith is **"the knowledge of God and of Jesus our Lord."** It can take work. In 2 Timothy 2:15, Paul says, **"Do your best to present yourself to God as one approved, a worker who has no need to be ashamed, rightly handling the word of truth."** In the King James Version, this verse opens with the command to **"study."** Studying must be intentional and takes work. Take time to get to know God better.

FIRM FOUNDATION
DEVOTION #2 - DR. RANDY T. JOHNSON

"Therefore, as you received Christ Jesus the Lord, so walk in him, rooted and built up in him and established in the faith, just as you were taught, abounding in thanksgiving." Colossians 2:6-7

One of the keys to growth is setting the right foundation. I recently had knee surgery and it is quite apparent to me the value of knowing my knee will not give out. If you have ever had ankle or knee problems, you probably know what I am talking about. A firm foundation is vital.

In our passage today, Paul uses the phrase *"rooted and built up in him and established."* The wording seems a little redundant, but I do think it gives a more descriptive picture of having a solid foundation.

Psalm 1:1-3 also envisions a tree that is very healthy due to being rooted and established, *"Blessed is the man who walks not in the counsel of the wicked, nor stands in the way of sinners, nor sits in the seat of scoffers; but his delight is in the law of the Lord, and on his law he meditates day and night. He is like a tree planted by streams of water that yields its fruit in its season, and its leaf does not wither. In all that he does, he prospers."* The foundation comes from being in the Word and letting the Word be in you. It is the concept of reading a passage and then letting your mind chew on it all day long as you go about life.

Matthew 7:24-27 gives a familiar story that clearly relates to having a firm foundation, *"Everyone then who hears these words of mine and does them will be like a wise man who built his house on the rock. And the rain fell, and the floods came, and the winds blew and beat on that house, but it did not fall, because it had been founded on the rock. And everyone who hears these words of mine and does not do them will be like a foolish man who built his house on the sand. And the rain fell, and the floods came, and the winds blew and beat against that house, and it fell, and great was the fall of it."* The foundation is crucial. Our thoughts, words, and actions needed to be based on what the Word of God directs. It should be from and for God.

As I write this, I am reminded of a hymn from 1787 by George Keith titled, *"How Firm a Foundation."* The first verse says it plainly:

> How firm a foundation, ye saints of the Lord,
> Is laid for your faith in God's excellent Word!
> What more can be said than to you God hath said,
> To you who for refuge to Jesus have fled?

CAPTIVE
DEVOTION #3 - DR. RANDY T. JOHNSON

"See to it that no one takes you captive by philosophy and empty deceit, according to human tradition, according to the elemental spirits of the world, and not according to Christ."
Colossians 2:8

I have enjoyed sports my whole life. I have experienced success as a player and as a coach. I have also been on the other side of the story. I hate losing. I hate losing more than I enjoy winning. After a victory, I forget to celebrate and immediately start thinking about the next event. However, after a loss, I mull over it for too long. Unfortunately, it can consume me. Through the years and maturity, I am realizing my identity and value are not determined by a scoreboard. I have found three interesting points on philosophy and competition.

- The best defense is a strong offense.
- Offense wins games; defense wins championships.
- Offense sells tickets; defense wins games.

In our passages for today, Colossians 2:8 starts, **"See to it that no one takes you captive by philosophy and empty deceit."** This passage emphasizes defense. We need to be on our toes and not let the enemy in. The word **"captive"** is also translated as **"spoil you"** (KJV) or **"cheat you"** (NKJV). These words are so important to realize how dangerous the enemy is. We need to make sure we are not flirting with the world. Romans 7:6 adds, **"But now we are released from the law, having died to that which held us captive, so that we serve in the new way of the Spirit and not in the old way of the written code."** This is such a powerful concept. He reminds us that we have **"died to that which held us captive."** The enemy is not our friend.

The battle is not just about defense. In 2 Corinthians 10:5, Paul gives a mindset of offense, **"We destroy arguments and every lofty opinion raised against the knowledge of God, and take every thought captive to obey Christ."** This is not a dodgeball game where we just avoid attacks. There need to be times when we pick up the dodgeball and throw it at the opponent. We do not need to just tolerate. We need to study the Word regularly in order to be fully equipped for the spiritual warfare that is and will take place. After reading the Word, get books or resources that address topics you are or could be facing. Spend time with other believers studying the Word to better understand it and how to share it with others.

The battle is not just about offense or defense and which one is more important. We need both! Finally, in 1 Timothy 6:12, we are told, **"Fight the good fight of the faith. Take hold of the eternal life to which you were called and about which you made the good confession in the presence of many witnesses."** Know why you believe what you believe. Be ready to use it in love.

SET YOUR MINDS
DEVOTION #4 - DR. RANDY T. JOHNSON

"If then you have been raised with Christ, seek the things that are above, where Christ is, seated at the right hand of God. Set your minds on things that are above, not on things that are on earth." Colossians 3:1-2

Think about what you are thinking about. In this passage, Paul tells us to **"set your minds on things that are above."** The key action is to **"set your minds."** This is true in so many aspects of life. A Titleist Pro V1 golf ball has 352 dimples on it. Some golf professionals encourage their students to focus intently on just one dimple when getting ready to hit a shot. Basketball coaches train their hoopers to choose their focal point of being either just over the front of the rim or just inside the back edge of the rim. This is true unless, of course, they are considering the bank shot. The backboard actually has a painted target measuring 18 inches vertically and 24 inches horizontally. Its purpose is to stress the importance of focusing. Bowlers are classified by those who focus on the pins versus those who pick an arrow that is only fifteen feet away from them. Either way, they stare at their target until after they throw. By the way, basketball players, golfers, and bowlers all hold their poses as they mentally block out all outside influences. The starting point and finishing point is to **"set your minds."**

Paul says that as believers we need to "set our minds" on things that matter to God. These things are eternal. They give purpose and value to our lives. To **"set your minds"** is not easy or natural. It takes intention as we turn from fixating on ourselves and looking to Jesus.

In Hebrews 12:1-2, we read, **"Therefore, since we are surrounded by so great a cloud of witnesses, let us also lay aside every weight, and sin which clings so closely, and let us run with endurance the race that is set before us, looking to Jesus, the founder and perfecter of our faith, who for the joy that was set before him endured the cross, despising the shame, and is seated at the right hand of the throne of God."** We need to realize how fleeting the things of the world are, set them aside, and start **"looking to Jesus."** This phrase can and should be the motto of our lives. **"Looking to Jesus"** (ESV) is translated several ways including **"looking unto Jesus"** (KJV), **"keeping our eyes on Jesus"** (NLT, CSB), and my favorite, **"fixing our eyes on Jesus"** (NIV, NASB). We need to start each day by asking what the Lord wants from us. Throughout the day, we need to seek Him. Also, as we finish each day we should focus on Him and evaluate how the day went.

Romans 12:2 explains this mindset, **"Do not be conformed to this world, but be transformed by the renewal of your mind, that by testing you may discern what is the will of God, what is good and acceptable and perfect."** It is a continual challenge to change our thinking. It is a process of growth as we look to the Lord more and more.

Philippians 4:8 also challenges us to think about what we are thinking about, **"Finally, brothers, whatever is true, whatever is honorable, whatever is just, whatever is pure, whatever is lovely, whatever is commendable, if there is any excellence, if there is anything worthy of praise, think about these things."**

PROOF IS IN THE "PUTTING"
DEVOTION #5 - DR. RANDY T. JOHNSON

"Put to death therefore what is earthly in you: sexual immorality, impurity, passion, evil desire, and covetousness, which is idolatry. On account of these the wrath of God is coming. In these you too once walked, when you were living in them. But now you must put them all away: anger, wrath, malice, slander, and obscene talk from your mouth. Do not lie to one another, seeing that you have put off the old self with its practices and have put on the new self, which is being renewed in knowledge after the image of its creator. Here there is not Greek and Jew, circumcised and uncircumcised, barbarian, Scythian, slave, free; but Christ is all, and in all." Colossians 3:5-11

Have you ever heard the phrase, "Proof is in the pudding?" I was disappointed to learn it had nothing to do with our creamy dessert. The phrase comes from the United Kingdom and refers to something more like a stew in a sausage. They would take minced meat, oatmeal, and whatever was in the kitchen and stuff them in a prepared skin or bag. Then it was boiled. It is said that no one knew if it was done or prepared correctly until they tested it by taking a bite. When someone tells me they make the best chocolate chip cookies, I feel I need to be the judge by tasting them. The proof is in the pudding.

This is also true of our Christian walk. It is not just an emotional or specially worded prayer that makes one saved. It is a change of heart. It is turning from serving self to striving to follow and serve Jesus in word and deed. It is a call to repentance. The best way to label a tree is to look at its fruit. Apples come from apple trees.

In Colossians chapter 3, Paul gives examples of how to live out our salvation. He uses the word *"put"* four times:

- *"Put to death"* - Paul tells believers to destroy habitual sin. The problem with habitual sin is that it begins to control us. It becomes our god. That is idolatry.
- *"Put them all away"* - Paul lists a few verbal forms of sin. James chapter 3 reminds us of the difficulty of controlling the tongue. However, as believers, our walk and talk must be consistent with each other.
- *"Put off"* - Paul lets them work on this by themselves. They are told to think about what they used to do and change. It is time to grow up. We need to "grow up" toward the Lord.
- *"Put on"* - We are to be a new person. We are born again. In 2 Corinthians 5:17, Paul says, *"Therefore, if anyone is in Christ, he is a new creation. The old has passed away; behold, the new has come."*

The proof is in the pudding relates in that just saying one is a Christian is weak. There should be proof in our words and actions that make it clear to others that we have given our life to the Lord. This does not mean we have to or even can be perfect, but we should strive to please the Lord in everything we do, say, and think.

LOVE
DEVOTION #6 - DR. RANDY T. JOHNSON

"Put on then, as God's chosen ones, holy and beloved, compassionate hearts, kindness, humility, meekness, and patience, bearing with one another and, if one has a complaint against another, forgiving each other; as the Lord has forgiven you, so you also must forgive. And above all these put on love, which binds everything together in perfect harmony."
Colossians 3:12-14

This passage is so beautiful. Paul gives a precious description of believers, **"God's chosen ones, holy and beloved."** This is rich with meaning. The Christian journey starts and builds through the love of God. God loves you! Pause and let that sink in. God's love gives us strength and purpose for the day.

Paul then gives a list of characteristics that we should wear as cherished clothes, **"compassionate hearts, kindness, humility, meekness, and patience."** He then gets more specific reminding us people will be difficult. We are to bear with them and forgive them. It will not always be easy, but it is simple. We are to love others. All of these traits can be summarized in love.

Love is obviously not a new concept. When Jesus was asked by the Pharisees what the greatest commandment is, He answered with love. Matthew 22:37-39 records His answer, **"And he said to him, 'You shall love the Lord your God with all your heart and with all your soul and with all your mind. This is the great and first commandment. And a second is like it: You shall love your neighbor as yourself.'"**

I appreciate Dwight L. Moody's perspective, "The world does not understand theology or dogma, but it understands love and sympathy." This is what Jesus was saying in John 13:35, **"By this all people will know that you are my disciples, if you have love for one another."**

All too often we respond as if love is just a feeling. Although love can make our hearts beat faster and our minds race with excitement, it is unseen or realized without action. Love is more of a verb than a noun. Love is something we do. As Christians, we are to love God and love others. This is not just to be found in our hearts and minds but needs to work itself out through our mouths, hands, and feet.

OUR MISSION

Matthew 28:19-20: *"Go therefore and make disciples of all nations, baptizing them in the name of the Father and of the Son and of the Holy Spirit, teaching them to observe all that I have commanded you. And behold, I am with you always, to the end of the age."*

REACH

At The River Church, you will often hear the phrase, "We don't go to church, we are the Church." We believe that as God's people, our primary purpose and goal is to go out and make disciples of Jesus Christ. We encourage you to reach the world in your local communities.

GATHER

Weekend Gatherings at The River Church are all about Jesus, through singing, giving, serving, baptizing, taking the Lord's Supper, and participating in messages that are all about Jesus and bringing glory to Him. We know that when followers of Christ gather together in unity, it's not only a refresher it's bringing life-change.

GROW

Our Growth Communities are designed to mirror the early church in Acts as having *"all things in common."* They are smaller collections of believers who spend time together studying the Word, knowing and caring for one another relationally, and learning to increase their commitment to Christ by holding one another accountable.

The River Church
8393 E. Holly Rd.
Holly, MI 48442

theriverchurch.cc • info@theriverchurch.cc

Made in the USA
Columbia, SC
26 July 2023

20911281R00065